DATE DUE		

Looking at

Animals in
COLD
PLACES

Published by Raintree Steck-Vaughn Publishers,
an imprint of Steck-Vaughn Company

Series Editor Honor Head
Series Designer Hayley Cove
Picture Researcher Juliet Duff
Map Artwork Robin Carter / Wildlife Art Agency
Animal Symbols Arlene Adams

Raintree Steck-Vaughn Publishers Staff
Project Manager: Joyce Spicer
Editor: Pam Wells
Cover Design: Gino Coverty

Library of Congress Cataloging-in-Publication Data
Butterfield, Moira, 1961–
Animals in Cold Places / Moira Butterfield.
p.   cm. — (Looking at —)
Includes index.
Summary: Describes some of the animals that live in the coldest climates of the world, including the harp seal, polar bear, snowy owl, Arctic fox, beluga whale, and emperor penguin.
ISBN 0-7398-0111-2 (Hardcover)   ISBN 0-7398-0714-5 (Softcover)
1. Mammals — Arctic regions — Juvenile literature.   2. Birds — Arctic regions — Juvenile literature.   3. Mammals — Antarctica — Juvenile literature.
4. Birds — Antarctica — Juvenile literature.   [1. Mammals — Polar regions.
2. Birds — Polar regions.   3. Zoology — Polar regions.]   I. Title.   II. Series:
Butterfield, Moira, 1961–   Looking at —
QL 736.B88   1999
599'.0911 — dc21   99-11583
CIP

Printed in China
1 2 3 4 5 6 7 8 9 0 LB 02 01 00 99

Photographic credits
BBC Natural History Unit: 26 Jeff Foott. Biofotos: 27 Brian Rogers. Bruce Coleman Ltd:
8 Johnny Johnson; 24 Jeff Foott; 28 Hans Reinhard. Frank Lane Picture Agency:
6, 11 Silvestris; 16 Kurt Ramseyer; 23 Brake/Sunset; 29 M. Horning/Earthviews. Planet Earth Pictures: 13 Geoff du Feu; 14 Frank Krahmer; 19 Mark Mattock; 21 Tom Walker. Oxford Scientific Films: 7 Doug Allan; 9 Dan Guravich; 10 Graham Wren; 12 E.R. Degginger;
15 Richard Farnell; 17, 22 Daniel Cox; 18 Michael Leach; 20 Tom Ulrich; 25 Zig Leszczynski.
Cover credit Emperor penguin: Bruce Coleman Ltd./Hans Reinhard

Looking at

Animals in
COLD
PLACES

Moira Butterfield

RSVP

RAINTREE
STECK-VAUGHN
PUBLISHERS
A Steck-Vaughn Company

Austin, Texas

www.steck-vaughn.com

Introduction

The coldest places in the world are in the far north and the far south. The north is called the Arctic, and the south is called the Antarctic. These are called polar places.

When it is winter in polar places, there are terrible storms and howling winds. The ocean is so cold it freezes over. Even in summer, polar places are very cold.

Some animals live in polar places all the time. Some animals visit only for the summer and leave in winter. All the animals in polar places have their own special ways to stay alive in the cold.

Contents

Harp Seal

Seals live in cold places where it is snowy and icy. Harp seals live in the Arctic, the far north of the world. The babies have white fur. As they grow up, the white fur falls off. Then, their new fur grows in gray. Seals dive and swim under water, so that they can catch fish to eat.

Polar Bear

Polar bears are big and strong, with sharp teeth and claws. They roam the frozen north looking for seals to eat. They can smell a seal from far away.

These bears have thick fur and fat to keep them warm. The mother polar bear teaches her young to swim in the icy water.

Lemming

Lemmings live in the Arctic. They stay out of the worst cold weather by hiding in underground holes. Sometimes they pop outside to look for plants to eat. When they are outside, they are in great danger because many other animals are hunting for them.

Snowy Owl

A snowy owl can swoop down to grab a lemming in its sharp talons. The owl's legs are covered in feathers right down to its toes. These feathers keep it warm.

The owl's white color is a good camouflage. The white feathers make it hard to see the owl against the snow.

Caribou

The caribou live in northern parts of the world in big groups called herds. They have thick coats to keep them warm. Their wide hooves help them to walk in the snow.

Caribou have antlers. Males sometimes use their giant antlers to fight each other. Caribou are called reindeer in some places.

Wolf

Wolves live with their families in groups called packs. They work together as a team of fast and fierce hunters. They chase and catch other animals, such as caribou. Baby wolves learn to hunt by playing pretend fighting games with their brothers and sisters.

Kittiwake

In spring kittiwakes and lots of other seabirds come north to the Arctic to lay their eggs. Thousands of the birds nest together in big, noisy crowds on the cliffs.

Kittiwakes make their nests from moss and seaweed stuck together with droppings. They lay two or three eggs.

Musk Ox

Musk oxen have shaggy, warm coats, so that they can stand freezing Arctic snowstorms. They wander around in small herds, looking for patches of moss and grass to nibble. Wolves may try to attack their babies. The oxen stand in a circle with the babies hidden safely in the middle.

Arctic Fox

In winter the Arctic fox has thick, white fur to camouflage it against the snow. In summer, when the snow melts, the fox's fur turns brown. Foxes can hear very well. When a fox hears a lemming making small noises, it will creep up on it and then quickly pounce.

Beluga Whale

The beluga is a white whale that lives in the Arctic Ocean. It lives on tiny fish that it catches in its mouth as it swims along.

Whales have lots of fat called blubber under their skin. This keeps them warm when they swim in freezing oceans.

Elephant Seal

Elephant seals look big and very fat because they have lots of blubber to keep them warm. When they are sitting on land, they look clumsy. But, when they are swimming in the ocean, they are graceful. On land they call to each other by roaring loudly.

Emperor Penguin

Emperor penguins live in the Antarctic. They like to leap into and out of icy seas. When a female lays an egg, a male carries it on his feet under a fold of skin.

When the chick hatches, it sits on the male's feet. This way it does not touch the freezing ice.

Where They Live

This map of the world shows you where the animals live.

NORTH AMERICA

SOUT AMERIC

☐ cold places

🦭 harp seal

🐻 polar bear

🐹 lemming

🦉 snowy owl

🦌 caribou

🐺 wolf

🕊 kittiwake

🐂 musk ox

🐈 Arctic fox

🐋 beluga whale

🦭 elephant seal

🐧 emperor penguin

30

EUROPE

ASIA

AFRICA

AUSTRALIA

ANTARCTICA

Index of Words to Learn